End of the Tunnel

Aubyn Sharp

Special thanks to my loving mother and father, along with everyone else who has supported me on this journey.

Before you begin reading, I have a few words to say.

What you are about to read is a project almost two years in the making. This collection of poems is dedicated to those who have felt. Those who have spent their lives alone. Those who have someone to love. Those who are hurt and those who are healing.

Your first steps are about to begin…

The first step you take

is always the hardest.

Embracing something new

and hoping for the best.

Telling yourself it's okay

to stumble and fall.

So long as you get up

and keep walking.

Until you reach the end

and see those stone arches.

Embracing the light

at the end of the tunnel.

The tunnel that is life

and the journey of recovery.

The Steps You Take
with Someone

If our heartbeats could make music,

I would play mine every night.

Hoping you would hear it,

and play along with me.

Our daily calls give me hope

and nights out make me smile.

Our texts make me laugh

and video chats give me peace.

Knowing I get to see you

even if it is from a screen.

A phone screen does so little

when I want to hold you.

A speaker pales in comparison

to your angelic voice.

The late night texts

wishing each other good night.

It's never going to be the same

as us being together in person,

but I cherish every phone call.

Every text message we send

and pictures of our outfits.

The things that keep me going

until we see each other again.

Hugging and smiling together,

ready for another adventure.

I can only hope you stay

and I find the strength to say,

I love you with all my heart

and have from the start.

From when you came into my store

and stunned me like never before.

Helping me break out of my shell

and the walls I knew too well.

Small talk leading to long walks

and adventures through the mall.

Laughing about the chaos

of crazed shoppers among us.

I can only hope you feel the same,

before I let you walk away.

You hold a piece of my heart

that I lost many years ago.

The piece that made me smile,

and pushed me further.

Made me see color in the world

besides black and grey.

Showed me how it felt

to love and be loved again.

You hold the piece of my heart

that made me feel human.

When you love someone,

you start to miss everything.

The sweater they always wore,

the trips to the bookstore,

the long talks in your car

not caring about the time.

You miss their warm hugs,

and smile when they see you.

It hurts to see them leave

but when someone loves you,

you know they always come back.

I took every wrong turn,

so we could be together longer.

So I could talk to you,

about work and home.

So you would hold my hand

just for a few more minutes.

So I could save one last kiss

under the midnight sky.

So I could say I love you

one more time.

You touch so many hearts

with your smile and laugh.

You put others before yourself

so you can make them smile.

Push yourself beyond limits

to be someone better.

Someone I have come to love

and write about with a smile.

Waiting for you to come home

and see you smile as you read this.

Wanting to hear about your day.

You found me broken

and chose to heal me.

I still bear the scars

and trauma from the past.

Yet you still love me,

and make my heart sing.

You put my heart back together

and saved what I once lost.

A smile, a sense of comfort,

a place to call home.

Cloudy days remind me of love,

and the beauty behind it.

A shadow that looms over us

blocking out the light of day.

It comes when we least expect it

and disappears when we accept it.

Raining down drops of future tears,

making me wish I had an umbrella.

This sounds like love may be a drag,

until you see the clouds disperse.

As the light shines on that one person,

and you beg for it to happen again.

Love resides in all of us.

It follows every car ride,

every walk in the park.

It laughs at the jokes we tell,

and smiles when we are together.

It pushes us closer

when we feel far apart.

It makes every night lively

and every day more colorful.

It knows what we want to say

and forces us to say it.

Love stands with open arms

just like when I fall into yours.

I count the seconds with you,

because our time is limited.

Cherish all our memories,

because it feels like you are here.

Your calm voice rings in my ears

and I can feel your hand in mine.

Your perfume lingers on my hoodie,

and it brings me closer to you.

When you are not in my arms

I still have our pictures together.

We may not be so far away,

but it still feels like an ocean.

One I will cross to be with you

every day.

You know you love someone

when they are always on your mind.

When you can imagine holding them

even when you are miles apart.

You cherish every memory

like it will be your last.

You feel your heart skip a beat

just by holding their hand.

You hold them close

because one day apart was too much.

You know you love someone

when you say those three words,

even if they already know.

The world is beautiful,

Because it made you.

Your quirks, your smile,

And laugh that lights up the room.

You talk about life after school,

And dreams of seeing the world.

No more dark thoughts or fears,

Because you took them away.

Replacing them with a smile,

And I never looked back.

I hold you close in tears,

Because you helped me feel.

I pray one day you find this and smile,

Because you know it is for you.

Along with the life we cherish together,

And our unwritten future.

I miss holding your hand

when we walk downstairs.

I miss our café dates

where we talk about school.

Life after graduation,

and our dreams in the end.

I miss seeing your smile

and your eyes light up with joy.

You are my biggest inspiration,

because even though I miss you

I know you feel the same.

The Steps to Take to Grieve

My car feels haunted

by your presence.

My phone is quieter,

because we never call.

My nights seem endless,

and days seem too short.

My mind feels so lost,

because it lost its guide.

My heart feels empty,

and it never will be full.

I told myself to let go,

because it hurts to hold on.

It hurts to see your face every night.

with your ocean blue eyes

staring into my broken soul.

It hurts to remember our first date

where we ran away from our friends

so we could be alone.

You blushed when I looked at you

and I could not stop stuttering.

So we held each other and swayed

to whatever slow song that was playing.

We knew it would not last forever,

but we tried our best to make it last.

I used to dream about us

and the time we'd spend together.

The stories we would tell our friends

about our adventures thus far.

Our late night conversations

wishing they'd never end.

But like all dreams,

we wake up eventually.

Reality starts to set in

and life goes on.

I still have the origami hearts

scattered across my room.

When I made them for you

for the weeks we spent together.

I started to take them down,

because it hurts to see them.

You never liked my music,

because it was always too loud.

You always teased me so much

until I started to break down in tears.

Then proceeded to do it again,

like it never bore a consequence.

You forced me out of my shell

with a crowbar you labeled "love."

Instead you made me feel insecure

and twisted my thoughts into knots.

You said you loved me,

but now I know you never did.

We used to be so close,

before life got in the way.

It pushed us apart,

but I still held on.

I still wanted to talk to you,

and make you feel better.

I strived to move on

knowing you will too.

You may read this and ask why?

Simply because I genuinely cared

even though it made my heart ache.

The heart is merely an organ,

but to many it is more than that.

It is what we follow into darkness

so we may find our light at the end.

What pushes me to write for you

and do everything to make you smile.

It skips a beat to match your own,

and sinks the moment you leave.

If it is so much more than just an organ,

then why was it so easy to break it?

Only fools rush into love

and know it will be okay.

Their heart speaks volumes

so loud that everyone can hear.

Their cheeks turn red like roses

and their smile never fades.

Everything seems perfect,

but you know it cannot be.

Only fools rush into love,

because love is never at first sight.

It is miles down the road

and you have only said hello.

You taught me how to love,

and I could only shrug.

As if love was some joke,

or another rumor or hoax.

Then I fell into your arms,

where I fell under your charm.

Taking all my pain away,

because I had nothing to say.

No witty comments or remarks,

just the subtle beat of my heart.

I look back on that day fondly,

Even though we left our love be.

Four months passed since we parted,

no longer broken hearted.

I have come so far

carrying my broken heart.

Started to join society again

and close the door on my past.

Until I get that feeling again,

your voice echoes in my head.

I start seeing ghosts of our past

wishing they would vanish.

Like you did months ago,

when we agreed to be friends.

I feel your presence around me,

but nobody else is here.

Your voice whispers through my ears

"Come on, just one more time."

You used to say as I played our song

swaying in the middle of our home.

Simpler times for simpler people

or so I tell myself at night.

It hurts to see you gone

and move onto better things.

While I rest in our broken home

regretting everything.

I cannot listen to music,

because it reminds me of you.

I cannot drive downtown,

because it makes me remember.

I cannot draw in my book,

because then I see your work.

I cannot write about love,

because you took that away.

I never wanted to write this,

but it won't stop screaming.

The pain I feel every night,

buried under a mask.

I try to force myself to cry,

but the tears never come out.

I keep feeling your ghost,

and it haunts me every night.

I just want a night of peace,

I just want my tears back.

Instead of resting on your shoulder

or the floor of your car.

I saw a future I believed in,

and you called it lies.

I still wanted to be there for you,

but you pushed me away.

We both hurt our hearts,

because of a past I held onto.

Well here I am moving on,

and I hope you can do the same.

I tried to help you,

but you just push me away.

I know what you went through,

but I have nothing left to say.

You are fueled by pain and stress,

and I feel it call out to me.

It leaves me in duress,

because terror is all I see.

It is a tough time in the world,

and with that I keep going.

Yet you do not have to be cold,

because I was merely trying.

I wanted to see the future,

so I kept dreaming of us.

A life in the city,

as artists making it big.

Writing to my hearts desire,

and you drawing with a smile.

The coffee brewing inside

with a sunrise in view.

A future I saw vividly,

but it was never meant to be.

I look back on the past

and let myself feel.

The tears I once shed

begin to rise again.

Hands start shaking

like they did back then.

Head feels heavy

from the burden of memories.

Until I start to breathe

and let my mind drift.

I open my eyes

to a world anew.

One of bright colors

and a life without you.

You had me at hello,

but lost me at goodbye.

You pulled me in with a smile

and I fell under your spell.

I fell in love with your charm

and found myself at rock bottom.

Suffocated by my anxiety,

and your harsh words.

It hurt to say goodbye,

but at least now I can sleep at night.

I glance at the pictures of us,

stained from the tears I shed.

Wishing you were still here

to tell me it will be okay.

That this pain is temporary

and things will get better.

Instead I sit here alone

writing this poem.

Hoping it brings me closure,

it did.

The Steps You Walk Alone

I am not perfect,

Nor do I want to be.

I am happy to be a reject.

Just like the rest of society.

The world sets a bar unreachable,

And expects us to care.

I would rather live while able,

And outlive this nightmare.

It haunts us with memories and guilt,

Because it wants us to feel something.

It wants us to smash the walls we built,

And break us until we give in.

Yet my pain makes me stronger,

Because it shows me my mistakes.

I will be your puppet no longer,

And I will value the choices I make.

I live with a thousand voices

and they all fight for the stage.

Begging to be heard

begging to be seen.

Instead they are drowned,

by my own screaming.

I look in the mirror in tears,

And start to wipe them away.

No longer can I lose to my fears,

Or let anxiety get in the way.

I fight with a hole in my heart,

Because I was wronged before.

Your twisted words tore me apart,

Because you were rotten to the core.

Yet here I am still fighting,

And you are nothing more than fear.

I carry a voice of lightning,

Because I know you can hear.

I wipe my tears of hatred and pain,

And walk away from the mirror.

Returning to my beautiful day,

Because my head feels clearer.

You will tremble soon before me,

And I will see the light of day.

I will overcome you, anxiety.

I go dancing with ghosts

in hopes they become real.

I fell their cold touch

wrap around my hands.

The dust kicks up around us

and the music keeps playing.

Our footsteps move swiftly

so much I feel weightless.

Until the music begins to fade

along with my partner.

One day they may stick around,

but for now I dance by myself.

It is 3 in the morning

and I cannot sleep.

So much noise around me,

yet why is my room quiet?

I fall to my knees in pain,

Surrounded by the tan walls of my
bathroom.

The noise gets louder and louder,

Like a siren constantly ringing in my ears.

I beg to make it stop as tears pour from my
eyes.

The ringing in my ears turn into shrill voices

Screaming my deepest regrets and flaws.

Taking deep breaths until my lungs give out.

I am in the middle of a storm

Sailing on a raft as the waves pull me under.

Drowning, gasping for air.

The loud cracks of thunder echo across the
sea

Waking up on the floor of my bathroom

Surrounded by a puddle of my tears.

The voices begin to fade away,

but I still feel the waves beneath my feet.

I look back on the days

Where my life felt empty.

The lonely nights I spent in my room

Writing poems I would never finish.

My mind more blank than the page

I hold my pencil, but it doesn't move.

It lacks the motivation of its wielder

As I struggle to find the words.

Unfinished just like all the rest,

And all I can ask myself is why?

Why is it so hard to write a few words?

Instead I chose to let my mind rest

And wait for the words to come back.

Now I come back to them present day

And the pages remain blank.

All I can feel is stress,

because life makes me depressed.

Its darkness holds my heart,

and I feel it being torn apart.

Knocking me on my knees,

with its cold grasp around me.

You try to help me breathe,

but your darkness beats me.

I push you away as you did before,

because my darkness breaks me more.

At least you got your desire,

so you can climb up higher.

Yet I fall to the bottom,

with a voice I cannot fathom.

Giving up because things got tough,

and my life feels not enough.

I am lost in a tunnel of thoughts.

Speaking to me at once.

It brings me to my knees,

As I scream down the hall before me.

Hoping someone would come by,

But I can't see past my teary eyes.

They keep calling for attention,

Which I simply cannot give.

If only I could give something,

If only I could truly live.

These are the thoughts I ponder away,

As for tomorrow lies the same day.

Down the tunnels I shall go.

Into the thoughts nobody will know.

I wake up paralyzed with fear,

Because the thoughts are all I hear.

Headphones in my ears,

And the sky looks clear.

The music guides me down the street,

And its calming tone puts me at ease.

No cars honking as I cross,

Or people crying about their loss.

The world shines brighter,

And the people seem nicer.

No conflicts or contradictions,

Or petty feuds and arguments.

No fights over small actions,

Or feuds about public reactions.

It made me smile from my mask,

Because it was a world I wish we had.

Then I took my headphones off,

And that world I knew was gone.

I feel like I am gasping for air,

And drowning in my own despair.

It leaves me feeling distressed,

Like I am supposed to be depressed.

To carry this burden on my back,

As it tells me everything I lack.

Expecting me to fall on my knees,

Because my sorrow is what it feeds.

I am helpless in my own mind,

Because I have nothing to leave behind.

All my insecurities beating me,

Praying, wishing that I would bleed.

It leaves me haunted and hollow,

Without a guide for me to follow.

I feel haunted by my own ghost,

Feeding off what I hate most.

I feel tremors beneath my feet,

as the darkness consumes me.

Its tendrils pull me in

and I feel my heart racing.

I try to gasp for air

In this dark despair.

Inhaling its toxic fumes

and let out a sigh of gloom.

It has taken control again,

you monster, depression.

Just a few more steps

I used to tell myself.

A few more steps

until I reach greatness.

Just one more day

and it will get better.

That was twenty days ago,

when will it get better?

Memories are a curse

when you only feel sorrow.

Moments from better times

scream louder than usual.

Visions of a better life

are all you can see.

You try to tell yourself

that you will feel again.

When you already do feel,

as the tears flood your eyes.

A pain resides in my chest,

and I feel shackles at my feet.

This burden weighs me down,

so much I begin to sink.

I run until my legs give out,

but it never feels enough.

I fall to my knees in tears

wishing for this pain to end.

A hand rests upon my shoulder

and whispers into my ear.

I begin to get back up

while their steps fade away.

Wiping the tears from my eyes

and repeating their phrase.

The road of life is paved with thorns,

but make sure you see the flowers too.

The Steps You Take to Heal

You will never truly heal

until you choose to remember.

Not with the intent to hurt

or bring you to tears,

but to look back on your past

and learn to laugh at it.

A story rests in all of us

and differs between persons.

Told by many people

in many variations.

Often told to make others laugh

and sometimes make us cry.

Told to bring others together

or drive others apart.

To heal the wounds left behind

or create new ones.

Regardless it is still a story,

one only you can truly tell.

Dear past me,

I hope this finds you well.

I know the world may seem scary,

and you fear every part of it.

Nights on the town seem pointless,

and work may be your focus.

Most days you'd rather be alone,

so nobody can see you write.

However, you have so much to see

and one day you will.

You will learn to love the nights out,

and share your work with others.

You will embrace the present

instead of dwelling on the past.

You will learn to love yourself,

at a time when you'd never expect.

Sincerely,

Present me

I see the world through a lens,

and always want to take a picture.

A picture that leaves me in awe

whether the scene is good or bad.

A beautiful array of colors and life

or a collage of black and white.

Truth is we take many pictures

with the lens we use every day.

Some we pin to a board,

and some we try to toss away.

We call these pictures memories,

and a story lies behind them all.

Life never will be easy,

but it will get easier.

You will fall often,

but learn how to rise.

You will doubt yourself,

and pick yourself back up.

You will face several fears

and become brave.

If the stars could smile,

would they smile at us?

If the moon could speak,

would it sing us to sleep?

If the clouds could feel,

would they start crying?

If we could simply listen,

would we ever understand?

So many what ifs,

but never a concrete answer.

If I could erase my problems

like words on a page,

then life would be easier.

If I could rewrite every part

until it pleases me most,

then life would be easier.

If I could outline my whole life

and tell my story word for word,

then life would be easier.

If I could live my life on my terms,

then I would not be living life.

I would be skipping the details.

It is okay to not be okay.

It is okay to cry in your car,

and scream out to sad songs.

It is okay to take a walk

when life feels heavier.

It is okay to confide in others

and spend time alone.

It is okay to sit on the roof

and stare at the stars.

It is okay to feel,

because that makes us human.

It hurts to be insecure,

because the voices never end.

Always screaming in your ear

until you give in.

Afraid of your reflection,

because it never looks happy.

Or asking the same thing,

because you are always unsure.

You learn to cover your ears,

but it still is not enough.

It all feels hopeless,

before another comes like you.

Covering their ears

wanting to help cover yours.

I always wait for future,

but never live in the present.

I always look out for others,

before I look out for myself.

I always worry about people,

when they don't worry about me.

I always live my life

like it depends on others.

Until I learned to move on

and walk this path for myself.

Embracing everything around me,

like my life depended on it.

I will make mistakes,

Because that is life.

I will feel lost sometimes,

Because that is life.

I will want to kneel and cry,

Because that is life.

Someday I will get back up,

Because that is life.

People call me lazy

for spending a day inside.

Where I can dream

of a future I want to see.

After days of constant stress

to keep up with the world.

While my flame slowly burns

and flickers like my health.

I rest it for one day

so it can burn brighter tomorrow.

The heart is a reckless thing,

Because it is always beating.

It never takes time to breathe,

and pushes us forward each day.

Onto a new adventure or path,

that brings new scars

or heals old ones.

It aches when we are sad,

and skips when we are in love.

As reckless as it can be,

we cannot live without it.

A smile goes a long way

when you know it is real.

The feeling of pure joy

that flickers in someone's eyes.

How it impacts everything

and everyone nearby.

Spreading like a plague

of utter happiness.

One we take for granted

in this world of darkness.

I wanted to write my thoughts,

so I could look back on them later.

I never wanted to fall in love,

because I feared getting hurt.

Life will always be terrifying

if you never take risks.

The ones you love most

will leave you eventually,

but their memories

will always rest in your mind.

This poem has no purpose

or deep meaning to uncover.

Just a chain of random thoughts

that keep me up at night.

Of all the time I spent

in this brief glimpse of life.

I spent in good company

with stories to tell.

I chased my furthest dreams,

and met my harshest nightmares.

I felt the pain of loss,

and the joy of gain.

Of all the time I spent

in this brief glimpse of life.

I feel no different,

but know I am stronger.

It hurts to write sometimes

because I am not good enough.

I say I lack inspiration

even though I am surrounded by it.

I tell others I am getting better

when I am barely getting started.

I try to pick up the pencil,

but it hurts so much to fail.

Like I am holding myself back

by perfecting my imperfections.

I keep making excuses

so I can avoid the truth.

I am just another scared writer

afraid to speak beyond the crowd.

Today that changes for good

because I will do better.

I will scream from the rooftops

and the world will know my name.

A trip down memory lane

like a film in black and white.

Memories that once left me in tears

now bear a smile on my face.

Days where I spent alone in my room

leading to nights out on the town.

Not a thought in my head

aside from how lovely the sky was.

The thrill of finding that one book

which held me together for years.

The feeling of my first heartbreak

and the strength it gave me overtime.

Thinking I would see credits after,

but there are so many scenes left.

This is just intermission,

and I await to see act two.

Once again, thank you for reading. I hope

you enjoyed my poetry and everything it has

to offer.

Follow me on social media for more great

poems @aubyn.s.poetry

www.ingramcontent.com/pod-product-compliance
Lightning Source LLC
Chambersburg PA
CBHW060037050426
42448CB00012B/3053